Latitude   >   44° 49'
Longitude >   20° 28'

F-14 TOMCATS

BY DENNY VON FINN

EPIC

BELLWETHER MEDIA · MINNEAPOLIS, MN

EPIC BOOKS are no ordinary books. They burst with intense action, high-speed heroics, and shadows of the unknown. Are you ready for an Epic adventure?

This edition first published in 2014 by Bellwether Media, Inc.

No part of this publication may be reproduced in whole or in part without written permission of the publisher. For information regarding permission, write to Bellwether Media, Inc., Attention: Permissions Department, 5357 Penn Avenue South, Minneapolis, MN 55419.

Library of Congress Cataloging-in-Publication Data

Von Finn, Denny,
 F-14 Tomcats / by Denny Von Finn.
    pages cm. – (Epic: military vehicles)
 Includes bibliographical references and index.
 Summary: "Engaging images accompany information about F-14 Tomcats. The combination of high-interest subject matter and light text is intended for students in grades 2 through 7"–Provided by publisher.
 Audience: Ages 6-12.
 ISBN 978-1-60014-941-2 (hbk. : alk. paper)
 1. Tomcat (Jet fighter plane)–Juvenile literature. I. Title.
 UG1242.F5V652 2014
 623.74'64–dc23
                                            2013002424

The photographs in this book are reproduced through the courtesy of the United States Department of Defense. A special thanks to the following for additional photos: JeP, p. 8; Frontpage, p. 11; Ted Carlson, p. 17; Choicegrphx, p. 21.

TABLE OF CONTENTS

F-14 TOMCATS

The F-14 Tomcat's engines roar to life. Its crew waits for the signal. Then the aircraft streaks off into the sky.

AIRCRAFT CARRIER

THREAT DETECTED

Tomcat Fact

F-14 Tomcats took off
from giant ships called
aircraft carriers.

The F-14 is defending its **fleet**. The crew spots something high above their **canopy**. It is an enemy spy plane!

The F-14 climbs to meet
the aircraft. The enemy plane
turns for home. It is no match
for the mighty F-14!

WEAPONS AND FEATURES

GUN

The F-14 was a U.S. Navy **strike fighter.** It served until 2006. It carried a large gun, bombs, and **missiles**. These weapons could destroy targets on the ground and in the air.

Tomcat Fact

The F-14's gun carried almost 700 bullets. It could fire 100 shots per second!

MISSILE

JET ENGINES

The F-14 was a **supersonic** aircraft. It had two **jet engines**. It could fly more than twice the speed of sound.

The F-14 had special wings. They swept back as the aircraft flew faster. This helped the pilot control the F-14 at high speeds.

F-14 MISSIONS

Two crew members went on F-14 **missions**. The pilot flew the F-14. The **radar intercept officer** was in charge of weapons and **radar**.

RADAR INTERCEPT OFFICER

213

17

The first F-14s defended Navy fleets. Later they attacked ground targets. They also helped spy on enemies.

VEHICLE BREAKDOWN: F-14 TOMCAT

Used By:	U.S. Navy
Entered Service:	1974
Length:	62 feet, 9 inches (19.1 meters)
Height:	16 feet (4.9 meters)
Maximum Takeoff Weight:	74,350 pounds (33,725 kilograms)
Wingspan:	64 feet (19 meters) unswept; 38 feet (11.4 meters) swept
Top Speed:	1,544 miles (2,484 kilometers) per hour
Range:	1,840 miles (2,960 kilometers)
Ceiling:	above 50,000 feet (15,240 meters)
Crew:	2
Weapons:	gun, missiles, bombs
Primary Missions:	air-to-air combat, air-to-ground attack, and fleet defense

Tomcat Fact

F-14 Tomcats starred
in the hit movie
Top Gun.

F-14 Tomcats saw action in Vietnam and the **Middle East**. The last F-14 mission was in 2006. Today the aircraft is remembered as one of the world's top fighters!

GLOSSARY

canopy—the clear, bulletproof covering over a cockpit

fleet—a large group of ships

jet engines—powerful engines that push a plane forward

Middle East—the region of the world located in western Asia

missiles—explosives that are guided to a target

missions—military tasks

radar—a system that uses radio waves to locate targets

radar intercept officer—the F-14 crew member in charge of weapons and radar

strike fighter—a small, quick military aircraft that destroys targets on the ground and in the air

supersonic—faster than the speed of sound; sound travels about 760 miles (1,225 kilometers) per hour at sea level.

TO LEARN MORE

At the Library

David, Jack. *F-14 Tomcats*. Minneapolis, Minn.: Bellwether Media, 2009.

Von Finn, Denny. *Supersonic Jets*. Minneapolis, Minn.: Bellwether Media, 2010.

Zuehlke, Jeffrey. *Fighter Planes*. Minneapolis, Minn.: Lerner Publications, 2005.

On the Web

Learning more about F-14 Tomcats is as easy as 1, 2, 3.

1. Go to www.factsurfer.com.

2. Enter "F-14 Tomcats" into the search box.

3. Click the "Surf" button and you will see a list of related Web sites.

With factsurfer.com, finding more information is just a click away.

INDEX